W9-BGS-836

DEFINING
MOMENTS

STUDY GUIDE

ANDY STANLEY

Multnomah Books

DEFINING MOMENTS STUDY GUIDE
published by Multnomah Books

© 2004 by North Point Ministries, Inc.
International Standard Book Number: 978-1-59052-464-0

Scripture quotations are from:
The Holy Bible, New International Version
© 1973, 1984 by International Bible Society,
used by permission of Zondervan Publishing House

Published in the United States by WaterBrook Multnomah, an imprint of The Doubleday
Publishing Group, a division of Random House Inc., New York.

MULTNOMAH and its mountain colophon are registered trademarks of Random House Inc.

Printed in the United States of America

For information:
MULTNOMAH PUBLISHERS
12265 ORACLE BOULEVARD, SUITE 200
COLORADO SPRINGS, CO 80921

08 09 10—12 11 10 9 8

Contents

DEFINING MOMENTS STUDY GUIDE
published by Multnomah Books

© 2004 by North Point Ministries, Inc.
International Standard Book Number: 978-1-59052-464-0

Scripture quotations are from:
The Holy Bible, New International Version
© 1973, 1984 by International Bible Society,
used by permission of Zondervan Publishing House

Published in the United States by WaterBrook Multnomah, an imprint of the Crown
Publishing Group, a division of Random House Inc., New York.

MULTNOMAH and its mountain colophon are registered trademarks of Random House Inc.

Printed in the United States of America

For information:
MULTNOMAH BOOKS
12265 ORACLE BOULEVARD, SUITE 200
COLORADO SPRINGS, CO 80921

11 12 13 — 12 11 10 9

Defining Moments

by Andy Stanley

L ife is full of defining moments. Right now, you are either facing a defining moment or between defining moments. Like landmarks on a map, defining moments mark the key points along your journey through this life.

There's a big difference between a life-changing experience and a defining moment. A life-changing experience is a shift in circumstances or events. It happens to you whether you agree with it or not.

But a defining moment is different. A defining moment happens when you come face-to-face with a truth about life that invites you to change the way you live. A defining moment demands a decision on your part. And once you reach a defining moment, regardless of the choice you make, your life will never be the same.

For the next several weeks we will examine several defining moments in the lives of key people in Scripture. And I think you'll agree that their defining moments parallel the ones you and I will experience in our lifetimes. Some of these encounters are with truths you've never heard before. However, many are truths you've heard but may have forgotten about or blocked out of your mind because you weren't ready to face them.

But as you're about to discover, when you're willing to look at truth honestly, it can be a moment in time that changes your life forever.

Sincerely,

Andy Stanley

Letting Go

INTRODUCTION

A defining moment often happens when a person comes face-to-face with a truth about life he's never confronted before. But if we're honest, most of our defining moments happen with truths we've simply been ignoring for a long, long time.

In fact, one of the main reasons people dismiss God's truth is that it's simply too painful or inconvenient to acknowledge it. We have our own way of doing things. And while truth may be true, it's often too disrupting to incorporate into our lives. So we shove it aside in favor of what's familiar and comfortable. In effect, we choose to live with a distortion rather than embrace the truth.

But the problem is that for every distortion about God, there is a corresponding consequence. And no matter how uncomfortable truth may seem, it's nothing like the discomfort we experience when the consequences begin to mount up. In the Bible, as people embraced the truths Jesus taught, their lives were transformed. And in this session, we'll examine how letting go of what's familiar can be the first step to experiencing a defining moment with truth in your life.

E X E R C I S E

In Your Dreams

Right or wrong, we all have a picture of what we want God to be like. For each of the following areas of life, describe how you wish God would orchestrate things:

■ In your finances:

■ In your career:

■ In your relationships:

VIDEO NOTES

From the video message, fill in the blanks:

1. Everyone has a picture of what they want
   _____ to be like.

2. With every distortion of truth about God, there is a corresponding _____.

3. One of the reasons Jesus came into the world was to explain _____ to us.

> " What comes into our minds when we think about God is the most important thing about us."
> —A. W. Tozer

DISCUSSION QUESTIONS

Take a few moments to discuss your answers to these questions with the group.

1. What are some misconceptions that people have about God?

2. What are some truths that you've seen people embrace or reject?

3. How have we attempted to shape God in our own image?

4. What consequences have you suffered by avoiding God's truth? What truths have set you free?

5. If a defining moment is embracing an uncomfortable truth, have you had that kind of defining moment?

6. Which truths that Jesus taught are the hardest for you to accept and why?

7. Which truths do you not want to face in order to avoid discomfort?

NOTES

MILEPOSTS

■ A defining moment happens when we come face-to-face with a truth about life and our lives are never the same.

■ Often, we shove truth to the side because it's too painful or inconvenient to acknowledge it.

■ For every distortion about God, there is a corresponding consequence.

WHAT WILL YOU DO?

1. Are there any areas in your life where you are putting off facing the truth? It could be a truth you have heard before but just weren't ready to incorporate. This week identify at least one truth that fits this description, and complete the statements below.

The truth I've been putting off is:

The distortion I've been embracing is:

THINK ABOUT IT

For every distortion of God's truth, there is a corresponding consequence. Are there any consequences you've already encountered as a result of putting off the truth? What consequences might lie ahead if you don't face up to the truth now?

CHANGING YOUR MIND

Replacing a distortion requires that we renew our minds to God's truth. You can begin by carrying God's Word with you throughout the day. There's a memory verse for each week. Begin memorizing them now.

Jesus said, "If you hold to my teaching,
you are really my disciples.
Then you will know the truth,
and the truth will set you free."

JOHN 8:31–32

We saw that truth is something we often choose to
ignore because it's simply inconvenient or too painful
to embrace. However, for every distortion of God's
truth, there is a corresponding consequence.
Therefore, God's Word exhorts us to hold to God's
teaching; in time, the truth will set us free.

Session 2

Good Isn't Good Enough

INTRODUCTION

One of the first truths about God a person must confront is the reality
of Jesus' identity. Throughout history, people have held a variety of different views about who Jesus was. Some say He was a teacher from
God. Others have said He was a prophet, a wise leader, or an example
of goodness for mankind to follow.

But in John's account of Jesus' life, Jesus presents a truth about Himself that has provided a defining moment for people for two thousand years. When you encounter this truth, there is no middle ground. Either you embrace what Jesus said about Himself, or you pursue a distortion that accommodates your existing beliefs.

In this session, we'll look at an eye-opening encounter between Jesus and a man named Nicodemus. In it, Jesus presents a belief system that resulted in a complete transformation of Nicodemus' theology. To embrace it meant abandoning everything he had been taught about God.

In a similar way, every man and woman faces the same defining moment Nicodemus faced. And like him, we must all make a momentous decision when we discover that "good" isn't good enough.

YOU CAN'T GET THERE FROM HERE

Around the world, there are literally hundreds of different beliefs about how a person gets into heaven. Take five minutes and list as many as you can think of.

Example: your good works must outweigh your bad deeds, you must be of a certain race, you must be baptized correctly, etc.

EXERCISE

VIDEO NOTES

From the video message, fill in the blanks:

1. Nicodemus was a member of the Jewish ruling

   _____.

2. Physical birth does not gain you entrance into God's

   _____.

3. Jesus said that we would never enter God's kingdom until

   we are _____ again.

4. You don't get to heaven by being good, but by placing

   your _____ in Jesus.

> " Salvation is completely
> unmerited (undeserved grace)
> but it is not unconditional. "
>   —John Piper

DISCUSSION QUESTIONS

Take a few moments to discuss your answers to these questions with the group.

1. Why do you think so many people are willing to accept only a portion of Jesus' message and blend it in with their worldviews?

2. Why do so many people believe that eternal life is earned?

3. Do you attempt to blend Jesus into your own way of thinking about God? If so, in what way?

4. In what circumstances of your life have you not been willing to consider something simply because it seemed too difficult? What were the consequences?

5. Jesus radically altered Nicodemus' view of God. How have the things Jesus said and taught altered your view of God?

6. Nicodemus was challenged with a truth that changed the way he looked at everything. What has been a truth in your life that has caused you to reevaluate the way you look at everything?

NOTES

MILEPOSTS

■ The Jews in Jesus' time believed that salvation was
achieved through keeping the laws of religion.

■ Jesus announced to Nicodemus that no effort on man's
part was capable of qualifying him to enter heaven.

WHAT WILL YOU DO?

Even if you've been a Christian for a long time, it can still be tempting
to think that your good works somehow improve your standing with
God. What works are you most likely to associate with bettering yourself with God?

THINK ABOUT IT

Have you embraced the truth that faith in Jesus is the only way to enter
heaven? What do you most remember about that defining moment? If
not, are you ready to embrace that truth today?

CHANGING YOUR MIND

Remind yourself of this important foundational truth by meditating on this verse throughout the week.

Just as Moses lifted up the snake in the desert,

so the Son of Man must be lifted up,

that everyone who believes in him

may have eternal life.

JOHN 3:14–15

LAST WEEK...

We examined the most important defining moment in

a person's life: trusting Christ for salvation.

As Jesus explained to Nicodemus, no one can see

the kingdom of heaven until he receives the

spiritual life Jesus offers.

Session 3

A Conflict of Interest

INTRODUCTION

Of all the things Jesus preached about, perhaps nothing is more disturbing and uncomfortable than what He said about money and possessions. To the rich, He often advised selling everything. To the poor, He suggested that they already had the greatest riches of all. Indeed, over and over God's Word points to an upside-down economy in which a person who loves his life will lose it, and a person who loses his life will receive eternal life in exchange.

Interestingly, the Bible says more about money than about heaven and hell combined. That's because of all the things God cherishes, He wants our devotion more than anything else. And God knows that nothing competes more for our affection than our pursuit and management of wealth.

In this session, we'll examine the story of a young man who found himself face-to-face with Jesus on this very issue. And in the process, he experienced a defining moment that exposed the true love of his life. As the key to our daily provisions, money plays an important role in the life of anyone who inhabits the earth. But as we're about to see, sometimes there's a fine line between what we own and what owns us.

WHICH WAY DID IT GO?

Nothing says more about a person's priorities than his calendar and his checkbook. If someone were to read your checkbook ledger, what would it say about your priorities? In the space below, quickly jot down approximate percentages of where your money goes each month. Discuss your answers with the group.

Food and Shelter _____ %

EXERCISE

Transportation _____%

Travel and Entertainment _____%

Savings _____%

Giving _____%

Other _____%

E X E R C I S E

VIDEO NOTES

From the video message, fill in the blanks:

1. God wants our love, our loyalty, and our

   _____-ship.

2. Nothing competes more for your love for Christ than
   your pursuit and management of

   _____.

> *Money never made a man happy yet, nor will it. There is nothing in its nature to produce happiness. The more a man has, the more he wants. Instead of filling a vacuum, it makes one.*
> —Benjamin Franklin

DISCUSSION QUESTIONS

Take a few moments to discuss your answers to these questions with the
group.

1. How do people use God to protect their "stuff"?

2. Have you experienced a "defining moment" with your finances? What was it?

3. Andy tells us that giving is the cure for greed. How has this principle played out in your life?

4. Why is the way you handle your finances a reflection of what's in your heart?

5. When you love, you prioritize accordingly. What are your priorities?

6. What needs to change in order for you to adopt God's view of possessions?

NOTES

MILEPOSTS

■ God wants our love, our loyalty, and our follow-ship.

■ Nothing competes more for your love for Christ than your pursuit and management of wealth.

WHAT WILL YOU DO?

Luke 12:34 explains that when we spend our money on something, its value and importance tend to grow in our minds: "For where your treasure is, there your heart will be also." This means we can train our hearts to love what we choose to love simply by "investing" in those things that should be our top priorities. This is a powerful principle we can use to make sure our possessions do not begin to own us. This week, give a special offering of money and/or time to God's work in order to ensure that your heart is being led in the right direction.

THINK ABOUT IT

The more time and money we invest in something, the more we tend to value it—whether it should be a priority or not. What are some examples of poor investments of time or money that have become "important" in your life as a result of this principle? How can you use this principle for your benefit, to begin elevating the priorities that are important to you?

CHANGING YOUR MIND

Affection is something that can be cultivated by fixing our minds on what we choose to make important. Train your mind with this principle by meditating on this verse throughout the week.

Now this is eternal life:

that they may know you,

the only true God,

and Jesus Christ,

whom you have sent.

JOHN 17:3

We learned that the pursuit and management of
wealth pose a huge threat to what is most important
to God: our devotion and loyalty to Him. Sooner or
later, every person must choose whether he will
serve God or money. And when he reaches that
crossroad, it will be a defining moment in his life.

Session 4

Seeing Is Believing

INTRODUCTION

Modern technology has caused us to think we're smarter than we are.
In virtually every arena of life, we can now explain things that used to
baffle our ancestors. So vast is our knowledge today that we tend to
think nothing is valid until we can explain it. As a result, many people
make the mistake of thinking they can't believe something unless they
have all the facts and can explain how all the pieces fit together.

But when it comes to matters of faith, that approach just doesn't work. We may be smart, but there will always be things about life, death, and heaven that we can't explain. And if we waited until we knew everything before we believed something, we'd never get anywhere.

Fortunately, Christianity is not based on a belief system anyway. It's based on an event that happened in history—Christ was crucified and raised Himself from the dead. In this session, we'll examine the story of a man surrounded by the unexplainable, yet confronted with the undeniable. And in that defining moment, as it is for us today, he had no choice but to believe.

I Don't Know About That

Examine each of the events below. In column A, write a percentage to indicate the impact each one has had on daily life. In column B, write a percentage to indicate the level of understanding possessed by the average person.

Scientific Event	A (Impact)	B (Understanding)
The development of antibiotic medicines		
The invention of the automobile		
Modern aviation		
The Internet		

EXERCISE

VIDEO NOTES

From the video message, fill in the blanks:

1. You don't have to understand everything to believe in

   _____.

> "" *It is my task to convince you not to turn away because you don't understand it. You see my physics students don't understand it.... That is because I don't understand it. Nobody does.* ""
> —*Richard P. Feynman, winner of the Nobel Prize in Physics*

DISCUSSION QUESTIONS

Take a few moments to discuss your answers to these questions with the group.

1. Give examples of things people believe but don't understand or cannot explain.

2. What are some things you believe that you don't understand?

3. What is a biblical truth you believe but don't understand?

4. How do the things you don't understand prevent you from trusting God?

5. What is an undeniable example of God's faithfulness in your life? In the last year?

6. In what area do you need to trust God even though you don't understand?

NOTES

MILEPOSTS

■ You don't have to understand everything to believe in something.

■ The more we focus on the undeniable, the less our faith is threatened by the unexplainable.

WHAT WILL YOU DO?

■ In the space below, list your top five "unexplainable" things about God, life, heaven, hell, the universe, etc.

■ Now list your top five "undeniable" things about Jesus Christ, including evidence of His presence in your life.

THINK ABOUT IT

Which part of the previous exercise strengthened your faith the most? How does this experience relate to the statement "The more we focus on the undeniable, the less our faith is threatened by the unexplainable"?

CHANGING YOUR MIND

Meditate on this verse to train your mind to the power of God's undeniable truth.

We proclaim to you what we have seen and heard,

so that you also may have fellowship with us.

And our fellowship is with the Father

and with his Son, Jesus Christ.

1 JOHN 1:3–4

We learned that it's possible to believe in

something without being able to explain everything.

And though we will always be surrounded by things

that are unexplainable,

we can fully trust in what is undeniable.

Session 5

Thirsty?

INTRODUCTION

Human beings have an amazing ability to cope emotionally. In the face of unimaginable pain, many people just grin and bear it. It seems we are taught from an early age that if we can just put the discomfort out of our minds, it won't hurt quite so bad. As a result, many of us go through life with emotional pain we rarely acknowledge, because it's just easier to endure the misery than to face up to it.

Meanwhile, Jesus invites us to experience an abundant life. He speaks of living water that quenches our thirst and satisfies our soul. But to drink of this water, we must first admit we need quenching. And that's uncomfortable.

You see, admitting we're thirsty means taking a risk. It means we can't ignore the pain anymore. It requires that we acknowledge our anguish long enough to lay it at God's feet. And as we'll see in this session, that's not easy to do when we've spent a lifetime learning to ignore our pain. At the same time, it can be a defining moment if we're willing to face the fact that we are thirsty.

TELL ME WHERE IT HURTS

In the space below, list the top three areas where you tend to thirst. Discuss your answers with the group.

EXERCISE

VIDEO NOTES

From the video message, fill in the blanks:

1. Jesus wants to put us in touch with our

   _____.

> " *Pain is God's megaphone
> to rouse a sleeping world.* "
> —C. S. Lewis

DISCUSSION QUESTIONS

Take a few moments to discuss your answers to these questions with the group.

1. Why do people strive to fulfill their thirst for God with other things?

2. Do you feel valued by God in spite of the mistakes you've made?

3. With what or whom have you tried to satisfy your thirst?

4. If asked today, what would you say you are thirsty for?

5. Do you believe that through Christ your thirst can be quenched? If so, can you count on Christ to meet all of your needs?

6. In light of that truth, how will the way you seek to satisfy your needs change?

NOTES

MILEPOSTS

■ Jesus wants to put us in touch with our thirst.

■ When we seek to meet our needs our own way, thirst results.

■ Only the living water Christ offers is designed to quench our thirst.

WHAT WILL YOU DO?

From the exercise in this session, list again the top three areas where you tend to thirst. Then describe how God promises to quench your thirst in each area.

Example: Finances—when I seek God's kingdom first, He promises to meet all my other needs as well.

THINK ABOUT IT

Why do you think the world's solutions for quenching our thirsts are so appealing? Why are they incapable of quenching our thirsts over the long-term?

CHANGING YOUR MIND

Study this passage to help you remember that only God can quench your thirsts.

Jesus answered, "Everyone who drinks this
water will be thirsty again, but whoever drinks
the water I give him will never thirst.
Indeed, the water I give him will become in
him a spring of water welling up to eternal life."

JOHN 4:13–14

We explored how we are designed to find satisfaction in Christ. However, often we seek worldly substitutes to fill the longings in our lives. But only Christ's living water can quench the thirsts of our soul.

Session 6

Easier Said Than Done

Please refer to session 6 in the Group Curriculum menu or part 7 in the Complete Messages menu of the DVD

INTRODUCTION

In *Moses in the Bulrushes,* Hannah More wrote:

> O sad estate
>   Of human wretchedness; so weak is man,
> So ignorant and blind, that did not God
>   Sometimes withhold in mercy what we ask,
> We should be ruined at our own request.

We may know what we want, but only God knows what we need. And in God's eyes, our spiritual state is much more urgent than the laundry list of requests we typically bring Him in our prayers. Even more than being thankful for our many blessings, we should be thankful that God faithfully pursues for us what we need, rather than what we want.

While our prayers tend to center around our physical comfort, God is more concerned about our holiness. Because where we see surface symptoms, He sees our root problem. In our eyes, we have relationship problems. In His, we have a sin problem. What we consider a financial problem, He views as a sin problem. And our health problems He sees as yet another consequence of living in a fallen world.

God cares about our pressing needs. But more than anything, He wants to address our *primary* need. In this session, we'll explore how the things we think are urgent may not be the things that are most important. And if we're willing to consider that God knows what we need better than we do, it can be a defining moment for us.

You Want What?!

In our childhood we dream of many things we want in adulthood. But over the years, our desires mature. In the space on the next page, list three to five childhood dreams that you're glad haven't come true.

EXERCISE

Why do we so often want the wrong things?

VIDEO NOTES

From the video message, fill in the blanks:

1. The paralytic's pressing need to be healed was not his
   _____ need.

DISCUSSION QUESTIONS

Take a few moments to discuss your answers to these questions with the group.

1. Why do people prioritize the urgent needs over the eternal ones?

2. Describe a time when you didn't get what you wanted,
   but got what you needed.

3. When have you been disappointed at God's answers to
   your prayers?

4. If you believed that forgiveness of sins is the greatest need,
   how would your priorities change? How would your
   prayers change?

5. How should God's forgiveness impact your daily life?

6. What needs to change about your perspective in order for
   you to see what you need the most?

NOTES

MILEPOSTS

■ The things we want the most are not always the things
   we need the most.

■ While we focus on surface problems, God is focused on
   our sin problem.

WHAT WILL YOU DO?

In light of God's concern about your holiness and His agenda for your
life, what are some things you should begin to be concerned about? In
the space below, list three to five godly concerns for your life that you
can begin to address this week.

THINK ABOUT IT

The more we want what *God* wants for us, the more we begin to work
with Him in our lives. What are some ways you can begin to align your
desires with God's?

CHANGING YOUR MIND

Meditating on Scripture is the best way to align your desires with God's desires for you. Carry this passage of Scripture with you this week as a reminder of your primary need in life.

"Which is easier: to say to the paralytic,

'Your sins are forgiven,' or to say,

'Get up, take your mat and walk'?

But that you may know that the Son of Man

has authority on earth to forgive sins...."

He said to the paralytic,

"I tell you, get up, take your mat and go home."

MARK 2:9–11

We learned that there's a vast difference between what
we want for ourselves and what God wants for us.
Our desires tend to be oriented around our temporal
needs. But God's desires for us come from an eternal
perspective. Instead of thinking only about our
physical needs, God is leading us to discover the truth
that our spiritual needs are a much greater priority.

Session 7

Playing God

Please refer to session 7 in the Group Curriculum
menu or part 8 in the Complete Messages menu
of the DVD

INTRODUCTION

Control is a double-edged sword. On one hand, it's empowering to be
given authority over certain arenas in life. But on the other hand, it can
be very troubling. Because with control comes responsibility.

Nevertheless, life teaches us to place a premium on acquiring additional control. We learn from an early age that there's a cause-and-effect relationship between performance and authority. And so the pursuit begins. Because with control, you don't have to depend on someone else for your well-being. With control, you are not at the mercy of another person to determine your fate.

But as we're about to see in this session, none of us is really in control at all. And the danger is that when we forget God is really the one in control, our lives become filled with anxiety and insecurity. We were designed to function best in a personal relationship with God in which we live as if all authority belongs to Him. To lose sight of that fact is to invite havoc into our lives. But to face that fact is to experience a defining moment that will change our lives forever.

ARE YOU A CONTROL FREAK?

Are you a control freak? Or do you enjoy letting someone else decide things for you? For each of the following scenarios, indicate your level of anxiety (0 being lowest and 10 being highest).

E X E R C I S E

Situation	Anxiety Level
Landing in a commercial airliner during a heavy storm	
Undergoing an outpatient surgical prodedure	

EXERCISE

Situation	Anxiety Level
Riding in the passenger seat of a car while someone else drives	
Losing your job because of factors beyond your control	

VIDEO NOTES

From the video message, fill in the blanks:

1. Pilate could find no basis for a _____

   against Jesus.

2. According to Jesus, all power comes from

   _____.

> " The greatest lesson I've
> learned in God's school is to
> let God choose for me. "
> —D. L. Moody

DISCUSSION QUESTIONS

Take a few moments to discuss your answers to these questions with the group.

1. In what areas do people feel they are in control?

2. Why do people crave control?

3. Are you a "control freak," and how does that play out?

4. Describe a time when you have given up control and found it liberating.

5. How would I respond if I were absolutely confident that God is in control?

6. In what area of your life will you relinquish control?

NOTES

_____
_____
_____
_____
_____
_____
_____
_____
_____
_____
_____
_____
_____
_____
_____
_____
_____
_____
_____
_____
_____
_____
_____
_____

MILEPOSTS

■ Only God is in control.

■ All power ultimately comes from above.

WHAT WILL YOU DO?

This week, examine the areas in which you are tempted to feel the need to control and take responsibility. In the space below, list the top three to five categories. What would it look like to recognize that God is actually in control in these areas?

THINK ABOUT IT

Why do you think God would want you to acknowledge His control in these areas—for His benefit or for yours? Explain.

CHANGING YOUR MIND

Carry this passage of Scripture with you this week to help you remember who is in control.

For there is no authority
except that which God has established.

Romans 13:1

We experienced a defining moment when confronted
with the truth that God is in control.
While we are tempted to see ourselves as powerful
in certain arenas, there is no authority except that
which has been given from above.
Acknowledging this truth in our lives frees us from
anxiety and insecurity and allows us to experience
the peace that passes understanding.

Session 8

Imagine

Please refer to session 8 in the Group Curriculum
menu or part 9 in the Complete Messages menu
of the DVD

INTRODUCTION

It's the ultimate defining moment. The one we're all aware of but all
avoid: One day our life on this earth will end. Time is running out. We

don't know how much time is left, but we know it won't last forever. It's an undeniable fact.

And like all defining moments, there's a lot we can't explain about death. But based on the undeniable facts, there are some very important conclusions we can draw that will impact us not only for the rest of this life, but also in the life to come.

In this final session, we're going to discover two key decisions we must all confront. And as uncomfortable as it may seem, if you'll stay in the light of truth long enough, your eyes will adjust to reveal some astounding things about what you should be doing with the time you have left.

SHOW AND TELL

The Bible teaches that one day all Christians will get to give an account of their lives before God. In that time, we will somehow share or recount the kingdom efforts we've made during our lifetime. When we do, we will experience satisfaction that we were a part of it and joyful humility that God worked through us. In the space below, list up to ten things about your life you can't wait to "show and tell" with Jesus.

VIDEO NOTES

From the video message, fill in the blanks:

1. Our _____ is running out.

2. What we do with the time we have left impacts what happens after this _____.

3. _____ gives us the proper context for life.

> *" All that is not eternal is eternally out of date. "*
> —C. S. Lewis

DISCUSSION QUESTIONS

Take a few moments to discuss your answers to these questions with the group.

1. Do most people live for today or with the end in mind?

2. How do most people feel or believe about a coming judgment?

3. How often do you think about how you should live?

4. Is your motivation for doing good to minimize punishment or to maximize rewards?

5. How do you feel about the truth that you will give an account for your life?

6. How should your life change since you will give an account for everything you do?

7. As a result of this discussion, what will you do differently with the time you have left?

NOTES

MILEPOSTS

■ Death gives us the proper context for life.

■ What we do with the time we have left impacts what happens after this life.

WHAT WILL YOU DO?

This week, think about how you will begin to live with the end in mind—knowing that your time is running out. In the space below, list at least five lifetime goals that you want to accomplish with the time you have left.

THINK ABOUT IT

If you could accomplish anything in the world for God's kingdom and you knew you could not fail, what would you attempt?

CHANGING YOUR MIND

The fact that our time is running out is something we tend to put out of our minds. And yet it is one of the most important truths to remember. Meditate on this verse to help you develop an eternal perspective for daily living.

For we must all appear before the
judgment seat of Christ,
that each one may receive what
is due him for the things done
while in the body, whether good or bad.

2 CORINTHIANS 5:10

LEADER'S GUIDE

So, You're the Leader...

Is that intimidating? Perhaps exciting? No doubt you have some mental pictures of what it will look like, what you will say, and how it will go. Before you get too far into the planning process, there are some things you should know about leading a small-group discussion. We've compiled some tried-and-true techniques here to help you.

Leading 101

BASICS ABOUT LEADING

1. **Don't teach...facilitate**—Perhaps you've been in a Sunday school class or Bible study in which the leader could answer any question and always had something interesting to say.

It's easy to think you need to be like that, too. Relax. You don't. Leading a small group is quite different. Instead of being the featured act at the party, think of yourself as the host or hostess behind the scenes. Your primary job is to create an environment where people feel comfortable and to keep the meeting generally on track. Your party is most successful when your guests do most of the talking.

2. **Cultivate discussion**—It's also easy to think that the meeting lives or dies by *your* ideas. In reality, what makes a small-group meeting successful are the ideas of everyone in the group. The most valuable thing you can do is to get people to share their thoughts. That's how the relationships in your group will grow and thrive. Here's a rule: The impact of your study material will typically never exceed the impact of the relationships through which it was studied. The more meaningful the relationships, the more meaningful the study. In a sterile environment, even the best material is suppressed.

3. **Point to the material**—A good host or hostess gets the party going by offering delectable hors d'oeuvres and beverages. You too should be ready to serve up "delicacies" from the material. Sometimes you will simply read the

discussion questions and invite everyone to respond. At other times, you may encourage others to share their own ideas. Remember, some of the best treats are the ones your guests will bring to the party. Go with the flow of the meeting, and be ready to pop out of the kitchen as needed.

4. **Depart from the material**—A talented ministry team has carefully designed this study for your small group. But that doesn't mean you should follow every part word for word. Knowing how and when to depart from the material is a valuable art. Nobody knows more about your people than you do. The narratives, questions, and exercises are here to provide a framework for discovery; however, every group is motivated differently. Sometimes the best way to start a small-group discussion is simply to ask, "Does anyone have any personal insights or revelations they'd like to share from this week's material?" Then sit back and listen.

5. **Stay on track**—Conversation is like the currency of a small-group discussion. The more interchange, the healthier the "economy." However, you need to keep your objectives in mind. If your goal is to have a meaningful experience with this material, then you should make sure the discussion

is contributing to that end. It's easy to get off on a tangent. Be prepared to interject politely and refocus the group. You may need to say something like, "Excuse me, we're obviously all interested in this subject; however, I just want to make sure we cover all the material for this week."

6. **Above all, pray**—The best communicators are the ones who manage to get out of God's way enough to let Him communicate *through* them. That's important to keep in mind. Books don't teach God's Word; neither do sermons or group discussions. God Himself speaks into the hearts of men and women, and prayer is our vital channel to communicate directly with Him. So cover your efforts in prayer. You don't just want God present at your meeting; you want Him to direct it.

We hope you find these suggestions helpful. And we hope you enjoy leading this study. You will find additional guides and suggestions for each session in the Leader's Guide notes that follow.

Leader's Guide
Session Notes

SESSION 1—LETTING GO

KEY POINT

For every distortion of God's truth, there is a corresponding consequence. This fact should motivate us to move out of our comfort zones and embrace the truth head on. One of the keys to starting this process is to recognize that oftentimes our problem is not ignorance of truth, but our unwillingness to face up to it.

EXERCISE—"IN YOUR DREAMS"

The purpose of this exercise is to encourage participants to begin thinking about what a distortion looks like. You may follow the examples Andy Stanley gave in the video message. Encourage the people in your group to make a "wish list" about God. Although farfetched, these suggestions can help us to see how subtly we make subconscious alterations to God's nature to accommodate our lives.

VIDEO NOTES

1. Everyone has a picture of what they want <u>God</u> to be like.

2. With every distortion of truth about God, there is a corresponding <u>consequence</u>.

3. One of the reasons Jesus came into the world was to
   explain <u>God</u> to us.

NOTES FOR DISCUSSION QUESTIONS

1. What are some misconceptions that people have about
   God?

   This question is simply intended to open up discussion
   about the ways we redefine God to suit our needs. As the
   leader, your main goal with this first question should be
   to encourage the people in your group to participate in
   the discussion. You may call on individuals, but avoid
   asking them to talk about themselves until they are com-

fortable. Encouraging them to comment on people in general can make the situation less threatening.

2. What are some truths that you've seen people embrace or reject?

This question is more specific than the previous one. The goal here is to identify some of the truths behind our common misconceptions.

3. How have we attempted to shape God in our own image?

This question raises the suggestion that distorting truth is tantamount to idolatry. Ask participants to comment on some of the motives that drive us to redefine God.

4. What consequences have you suffered by avoiding God's truth? What truths have set you free?

We all have stories to share about the consequences of ignoring truth. Likewise, there are truths that have set us free. Recounting a few of these stories together should help everyone to visualize the main points of this session.

5. If a defining moment is embracing an uncomfortable truth, have you had that kind of defining moment?

Encourage the people in your group to recall specific times in their lives that they would consider "defining moments." Be ready to distinguish between defining moments and life-changing experiences. The former always requires a decision, while the latter does not.

6. Which truths that Jesus taught are the hardest for you to accept and why?

Each person in the group should identify the truth from Scripture they find most challenging and explain why.

7. Which truths do you not want to face in order to avoid discomfort?

Expounding on the previous question, encourage participants to discuss some of the discomforts that make God's truths difficult to embrace.

WHAT WILL YOU DO?

The goal of this assignment is to get participants to identify a specific truth that they need to address. If they're honest, chances are good that everyone will recognize a clear prompting to correct an old distortion.

THINK ABOUT IT

This part of the exercise is intended to provide motivation. When we are honest about the consequences of our choices in life, it's much easier to see the rationale of pursuing truth.

SESSION 2—GOOD ISN'T GOOD ENOUGH

KEY POINT

This session lays an important foundation for the rest of this series. The cornerstone of all defining moments is the decision to embrace the truth that salvation comes only through faith in Jesus. Nicodemus' encounter with Jesus (John 3) provides several important insights for us today. As Jesus explained to this member of the Jewish ruling council, only those who experience spiritual birth in Christ will see the kingdom of heaven. This position is offensive to some and causes many to turn away because it makes them uncomfortable. But as Nicodemus demonstrates, if we are willing to stop and consider God's truth, it can lead to a better understanding of the truth and freedom in Jesus.

EXERCISE—"YOU CAN'T GET THERE FROM HERE"

The point of this exercise is to help participants notice the many different beliefs about heaven that exist in the world. Some may seem strange and obscure. At the same time, some may observe that these beliefs often slip subtly into the worldview of some Christians. Anytime we try to add our efforts to Jesus' righteousness, we are embracing a distortion of the truth that only faith in Jesus saves us.

VIDEO NOTES

From the video message, fill in the blanks:

1. Nicodemus was a member of the Jewish ruling <u>council</u>.

2. Physical birth does not gain you entrance into God's <u>kingdom</u>.

3. Jesus said that we would never enter God's kingdom until we are <u>born</u> again.

4. You don't get to heaven by being good, but by placing your <u>faith</u> in Jesus.

NOTES FOR DISCUSSION QUESTIONS

1. Why do you think so many people are willing to accept only a portion of Jesus' message and blend it in with their worldviews?

The purpose of this question is to expose some of the underlying motives that drive us to resist the pure teaching of Scripture.

2. Why do so many people believe that eternal life is earned?

This question is intended to point out how the messages we hear in everyday life—in the media and in various social arenas—tend to shape our beliefs about God. Only the Bible is reliable for aligning our beliefs with God's truth.

3. Do you attempt to blend Jesus into your own way of thinking about God? If so, in what way?

Each of us has areas in which we tend to make God into our own image. This question prompts participants to reveal the areas in which we are most likely to drift from God's truth.

4. In what circumstances of your life have you not been willing to consider something simply because it seemed too difficult? What was the consequence?

For most people, spiritual growth is a gradual process of embracing new truths of God. That means there are truths we've resisted along the way. This question will help participants evaluate how this process works in their own lives.

5. Jesus radically altered Nicodemus' view of God. How have the things Jesus said and taught altered your view of God?

This question provides an opportunity for the people in your group to share how they have been able to embrace God's truth in their lives.

6. Nicodemus was challenged with a truth that changed the way he looked at everything. What has been a truth in your life that has caused you to reevaluate the way you look at everything?

When we embrace God's truth, the impact is inevitable. This question encourages participants to discuss the far-reaching effects of following God's truth in our lives.

WHAT WILL YOU DO?

This assignment is important for Christians and non-Christians alike. For Christians, it is important to fully embrace the theology of grace, not grace plus works. For non-Christians, it is important to understand the truth about salvation through faith in Jesus.

THINK ABOUT IT

Sometimes the details of a person's salvation experience are vague. And other times, there's an outright misunderstanding of what is required for salvation. This assignment is intended to make sure that everyone in your group has thoroughly understood and experienced salvation. The more details we can recall about our salvation experience, the more assurance we carry with us throughout life.

SESSION 3—A CONFLICT OF INTEREST

KEY POINT

Anytime our true motives are exposed, it constitutes a defining moment. The pursuit of money is often the seducer of our motives, quietly stealing our devotion away from God. Sooner or later, everyone must choose whether he will serve God or money.

EXERCISE—"WHICH WAY DID IT GO?"

The first step to aligning our lives with God's priorities is to take an honest look at how we live. This exercise is designed to reveal our priorities. Consider how you might challenge the people in your group to examine their choice of lifestyle—whether it supports their beliefs or forces them to neglect some priorities that are important to them.

VIDEO NOTES

From the video message, fill in the blanks:

1. God wants our love, our loyalty, and our <u>follow</u>-ship.

2. Nothing competes more for your love for Christ than your pursuit and management of <u>wealth</u>.

NOTES FOR DISCUSSION QUESTIONS

1. How do people use God to protect their "stuff"?

   This question suggests that our interest in God is often a disguise for our true interest: what God can do for us. If we're honest, we may discover that we have much in common with the rich young ruler.

2. Have you experienced a "defining moment" with your finances? What was it?

   This question is meant to encourage participants to share their experiences and insights pertaining to God and finances. Some of these defining moments may recount bad decisions about money; others may represent good ones.

3. Andy tells us that giving is the cure for greed. How has this principle played out in your life?

    Recounting expressions of generosity can be very motivating. This question will cause participants to examine the attitudes that are cultivated when giving is prioritized.

4. Why is the way you handle your finances a reflection of what's in your heart?

    This question brings to the surface the fact that money has the power to direct a person's heart. If we give, it tends to make us more giving. If we consume, it tends to make us more consuming.

5. When you love, you prioritize accordingly. What are your priorities?

    Similar to the opening exercise in this session, this question is an invitation for personal examination of where our priorities should lie.

6. What needs to change in order for you to adopt God's
   view of possessions?

   In light of where you'd like to be, what one or two steps
   can you take to begin moving toward the priorities you
   want your life to reflect?

WHAT WILL YOU DO?

Encourage everyone in your group to follow through on this assignment. If they do, it can truly cultivate a spirit of generosity, or at the
very least reverse the pull of greed. In either case, it will cause participants to ponder where their values lie.

THINK ABOUT IT

If you stop and think about it, we all serve habits and pastimes that
don't necessarily represent our priorities. Oftentimes, they creep into
our lives as the result of cultural influences or because of a lack of inten-
tionality on our part. Once we're involved, the tendency is for us to
remain involved and for our interest to continue growing.

SESSION 4—SEEING IS BELIEVING

KEY POINT

It is a defining moment when a person realizes that it is not necessary to understand everything in order to believe in something. When we focus on what is undeniable, our faith is not threatened by what is unexplainable. Even though we cannot explain everything about God, life, death, and heaven, we can still have confidence that Jesus is Lord.

EXERCISE—"I DON'T KNOW ABOUT THAT"

The purpose of this exercise is to demonstrate how our belief in something does not depend on our ability to explain it.

VIDEO NOTES

From the video message, fill in the blanks:

1. You don't have to understand everything to believe in <u>something</u>.

NOTES FOR DISCUSSION QUESTIONS

1. Give examples of things people believe but don't understand or cannot explain.

   Similar to the exercise, there are many things we believe in without fully understanding. This question is phrased so as to prompt general observations about people in general.

2. What are some things you believe that you don't understand?

   This question is phrased to elicit a more personal response.

3. What is a biblical truth you believe but don't understand?

   This version of the same question focuses specifically on scriptural beliefs.

4. How do the things you don't understand prevent you from trusting God?

We fail to trust God when we focus more on what is unexplainable than what is undeniable.

5. What is an undeniable example of God's faithfulness in your life? In the last year?

Everyone has examples of the "undeniable" in his life. This question is designed to encourage participants to focus on them.

6. In what area do you need to trust God even though you don't understand?

This question is designed to challenge participants to acknowledge areas where their faith has been limited because they are unwilling to trust unless they first understanding everything.

WHAT WILL YOU DO?

This assignment will help participants identify the exact issues that they find difficult to accept. It will also provide evidence to encourage faith in spite of them.

THINK ABOUT IT

This follow-up exercise drives home the point that faith is often a simple matter of perspective—when we focus on what is true, faith is not far behind.

SESSION 5—THIRSTY?

KEY POINT

Many of our deepest longings go unanswered when we continue the habit of trying to fill them with substitutes for God. It can be a defining moment when we face the fact that we are thirsty, and that only God can quench our thirst.

EXERCISE—"TELL ME WHERE IT HURTS"

This exercise invites participants to identify the areas where they thirst the most. Thirst is almost always an indication that some substitute has taken the place of God's presence.

VIDEO NOTES

From the video message, fill in the blanks:

1. Jesus wants to put us in touch with our <u>thirst</u>.

NOTES FOR DISCUSSION QUESTIONS

1. Why do people strive to fulfill their thirst for God with other things?

   This question points right to the motives that cause us to miss God in the midst of our need.

2. Do you feel valued by God in spite of the mistakes you've made?

   When we truly understand that God pursues us in order to quench our thirsts, we can't help becoming aware of how much He values us.

3. With what or whom have you tried to satisfy your thirst?

   This question will prompt the people in your group to discover their own patterns of seeking substitutes instead of God.

4. If asked today, what would you say you are thirsty for?

When we greet one another with, "How's it going?" most of us simply say, "Fine." This question is an invitation to examine whether there are any thirsts we have overlooked out of habit.

5. Do you believe that through Christ your thirst can be quenched? If so, can you count on Christ to meet all of your needs?

It is important for us to consider whether we truly believe Christ is the One who can quench all our thirsts. If we don't, we will never truly seek Him instead of our substitutes.

6. In light of that truth, how will the way you seek to satisfy your needs change?

The purpose of this question is to point participants toward specific ways to apply this session's message.

WHAT WILL YOU DO?

The purpose of this assignment is to probe deeper into the hidden ways in which substitutes creep into our daily lives. When we examine the promises of Scripture, it suddenly becomes clear how God has designed us to be satisfied only in Him.

THINK ABOUT IT

There are many reasons we drift from the truth. Some are the designs of the enemy, while some are caused by the frailty of our flesh. In either case, this exercise will help participants understand some of the patterns that leave us thirsty.

SESSION 6—EASIER SAID THAN DONE

Please refer to session 6 in the Group Curriculum
menu or part 7 in the Complete Messages menu
of the DVD

KEY POINT

We ask God for many things. But often, Christians are oblivious to what is really important in their lives. We may know what we want, but only God truly knows what we need. Beneath our surface desires is a set of eternal needs that God seeks to address in our lives. When we realize the truth that there's more to this life than what we want, it can be a defining moment for us.

EXERCISE—"YOU WANT WHAT?!"

This exercise will reveal how our desires shift over the years. Our wants are limited by our human perspective. But God has the advantage of an omniscient perspective when He views our lives. We should begin to prioritize the things He wants for us over the temporal things we think we want.

VIDEO NOTES

From the video message, fill in the blanks:

1. The paralytic's pressing need to be healed was not his <u>primary</u> need.

NOTES FOR DISCUSSION QUESTIONS

1. Why do people prioritize the urgent needs over the eternal ones?

   This question is intended to start conversation, as well as to point out our natural tendency to focus on temporal things instead of eternal things.

2. Describe a time when you didn't get what you wanted, but got what you needed.

   Often, the prayers we think are unanswered are actually answered with what we need instead of what we want. This question will help participants review their unanswered prayers and begin to see how God was at work behind the scenes.

3. When have you been disappointed at God's answers to your prayers?

   Disappointment is common as we grow in faith. This question will help the people in your group reconsider whether they should be disappointed or trusting next time they don't get what they want.

4. If you believed that forgiveness of sins is the greatest need, how would your priorities change? How would your prayers change?

   This question is important because it encourages participants to visualize how they should respond to this session's message. As the question suggests, we should have an eternal perspective when we pray.

5. How should God's forgiveness impact your daily life?

   In the busyness of each day, it's easy to forget our most important foundation. This question will help participants remember that everything we do should stem from our identity in Christ and the forgiveness He gives.

6. What needs to change about your perspective in order for you to see what you need the most?

As a final point, this question will help the people in your group to identify specific action points to begin applying this message to their lives.

WHAT WILL YOU DO?

As a part of our daily perspective, it's important to be aware of God's agenda. This assignment will help participants think of specific objectives that God thinks are important. As a result of this assignment, each person should be able to identify several new spiritual goals.

THINK ABOUT IT

It's one thing to become aware of God's current priority for us. But it's even more valuable to learn how to be aware of God's intentions all the time. Perhaps the most important thing a Christian can do is to develop a lifestyle of seeking God's will in each moment.

SESSION 7: PLAYING GOD

Please refer to session 7 in the Group Curriculum
menu or part 8 in the Complete Messages menu
of the DVD

KEY POINT

It's tempting to think that we are in control in certain areas of our lives. But the truth is that God is always in control of all things. Recognizing this truth can be a defining moment, freeing us from anxiety and helping us to discover the peace that comes from knowing God will work all things together for good.

EXERCISE—"ARE YOU A CONTROL FREAK?"

The purpose of this exercise is to give participants a visual picture of what it looks like to want control over things that are not ours to control. At the same time, it suggests what it should look like when we have acknowledged that God is actually in control.

VIDEO NOTES

From the video message, fill in the blanks:

1. Pilate could find no basis for a <u>charge</u> against Jesus.

2. According to Jesus, all power comes from <u>above</u>.

NOTES FOR DISCUSSION QUESTIONS

1. In what areas do people feel they are in control?

   The purpose of this question is to surface some of the common situations in which people are lured into exercising control. When we feel we are in control, we cannot feel God's control; they are mutually exclusive.

2. Why do people crave control?

   Before we can relinquish control, it helps to understand why it is appealing to us in the first place. This question should raise several important insights into why being in control holds our interest.

3. Are you a "control freak" and how does that play out?

   This may prove to be a challenging question for some. It may be difficult to admit, or even to see one's own tendencies. It may help to identify areas that make us feel anxious or insecure—these often indicate a struggle for control.

4. Describe a time when you have given up control and found it liberating.

Even if some participants are unable to recall a specific experience of their own, it will be encouraging to hear examples from others in the group. The main point of this question is to provide examples to demonstrate that peace increases when control decreases.

5. How would I respond if I were absolutely confident that God is in control?

The point of this question is to elicit some soul-searching. In response to this question, each person should begin to envision the ideal way to live in every given moment—as if God is the only one in control.

6. In what area of your life will you relinquish control?

The purpose of this question is to narrow this message
down to one or two specific application points. Encourage
the people in your group to commit themselves to imple-
menting these points this week.

WHAT WILL YOU DO?

This assignment is designed to dig deeper into possible areas in which
we need to acknowledge God's control in our lives. Encourage participants to approach this exercise prayerfully. If we are willing to admit
that we've been pursuing control in areas that actually belong to God,
it can be a defining moment in our lives.

THINK ABOUT IT

This part of the assignment is intended to remind us that God's main
goal is to help us begin living with an eternal perspective. As we mature
in Christ, our lives will reflect His nature and truth more and more.
Central to this effort is the notion that God is all-powerful and lovingly
in charge of every detail in our universe and in our lives.

SESSION 8: IMAGINE

Please refer to session 8 in the Group Curriculum
menu or part 9 in the Complete Messages menu
of the DVD

KEY POINT

The ultimate defining moment for all of us is the fact that our time on this earth is running out. It's an undeniable truth. And yet most of us avoid thinking about it. If we are willing to confront this truth head on, it will change dramatically what we do with our remaining days.

EXERCISE—"SHOW AND TELL"

One of the best ways to begin living for the future is to picture what it will look like when we get there. The purpose of this exercise is to force us to evaluate whether we've been living with an eternal perspective. Regardless of where a person stands, this can be very motivating.

VIDEO NOTES

From the video message, fill in the blanks:

1. Our <u>time</u> is running out.

2. What we do with the time we have left impacts what happens after this <u>life</u>.

3. <u>Death</u> gives us the proper context for life.

NOTES FOR DISCUSSION QUESTIONS

1. Do most people live for today or with the end in mind?

   Obviously, there is no right or wrong answer to this question. The main purpose of this question is to begin the process of examining the difference between living for today and living for eternity.

2. How do most people feel or believe about a coming judgment?

   If we're honest, most of us are uncomfortable with the idea of eternity, primarily because there is so much we don't know about it. The main point to be made is that regardless of what we feel or believe, the final judgment is coming.

3. How often do you think about how you should live?

The answers to this question may vary from person to person. The main goal of this question is to make us aware of how little most of us focus on a topic of such great importance.

4. Is your motivation for doing good to minimize punishment or to maximize rewards?

Many Christians fail to pursue rewards because they equate it with trying to earn salvation. This question will help distinguish between working to pay for sin and working to earn rewards.

5. How do you feel about the truth that you will give an account for your life?

This can be a revealing question for people. If we really consider the fact that we will give an account for our lives, it's easier to envision what we should be doing to prepare for it.

6. How should your life change since you will give an account for everything you do?

   The purpose of this question is to expose current practices, behaviors, or habits that will not enhance a person's eternity. In addition, it will help reveal those practices that, if incorporated, would help us prepare for life in eternity.

7. As a result of this discussion, what will you do differently with the time you have left?

   As a follow-up to the previous question, this question is designed to focus on specific action steps that participants can take as a result of this session.

WHAT WILL YOU DO?

With the final destination of eternity in mind, it is helpful to think in terms of setting goals for the time remaining. Being intentional in our approach to the future will help ensure that the outcome meets with our desires. The best defense is a good offense.

THINK ABOUT IT

This part of the assignment helps to suggest that when we think about the future, we should think about making the most of our opportunities, remembering that with God working through us, there is literally no limit to what He can accomplish in our lives. By posing this question, participants will be encouraged to consider possibilities they may not have considered otherwise.

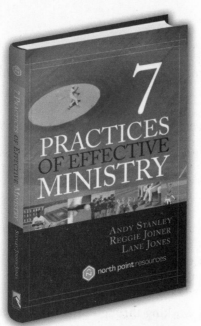

7 Practices of Effective Ministry
by Andy Stanley, Reggie Joiner, and Lane Jones
ISBN 1-59052-373-3

Rethink Your Ministry Game Plan
Succeeding in sports means victory, winning! But what does it mean in your ministry? An insightful and entertaining parable for every church leader who yearns for a more simplified approach to ministry.

Creating Community
by Andy Stanley and Bill Willits
ISBN 1-59052-396-2

Form Small Groups That Succeed
To build a healthy, thriving small-group environment you need a plan. Here are five proven principles from one of the most successful small-group ministry churches in the country. Learn them, implement them, and empower God's people to truly do life together.

north point resources

Parental Guidance Required
by Andy Stanley and Reggie Joiner
DVD: ISBN 1-59052-378-4
Study Guide: ISBN 1-59052-381-4

Influence Your Child's Future
Our lives are shaped by relationships, experiences, and decisions. Therefore, our priority as parents should be to enhance our child's relationship with us, advance our child's relationship with God, and influence our child's relationship with those outside the home.

Discovering God's Will
by Andy Stanley
DVD: ISBN 1-59052-380-6
Study Guide: ISBN 1-59052-379-2

Make Decisions with Confidence
God has a personal vision for your life and He wants you to know it even more than you do. Determining God's will can be a difficult process, especially when we need to make a decision in a hurry. In this series Andy Stanley leads us through God's providential, moral, and personal will.

The Best Question Ever
by Andy Stanley
DVD: ISBN 1-59052-463-2
Study Guide: ISBN 1-59052-462-4

Foolproof Your Life
When it comes to sorting out the complexities of each unique situation we face, only wisdom can reveal the best path. The question posed here will empower you to make regretless decisions every time.

 north point resources

Taking Care of Business
by Andy Stanley
DVD: ISBN 1-59052-492-6
Study Guide: ISBN 1-59052-491-8

Finding God at Work
God created work and intends for us to make the most of it! Gain His perspective and get equipped to make changes that allow you to thrive in the workplace.

Life Rules
by Andy Stanley
DVD: ISBN 1-59052-494-2
Study Guide: ISBN 1-59052-493-4

Instructions for Life
God's guidelines for living are for your protection and freedom. Learn them, live by them, and experience the dramatic, positive change in every area of your life.

north point resources

Best Question Ever
by Andy Stanley

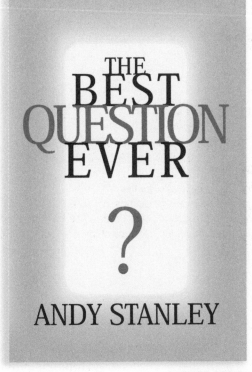

1-59052-390-3

Can you think of a question that has the potential to foolproof your relationships, your marriage, your finances, even your health? A question that, had you asked it and followed its leading, would have enabled you to avoid your greatest regret? Read *The Best Question Ever* to find out how to foolproof your life.